USUAL
A Ghost Most Unusual

An Unscary Story About Kids Behaving Oddly

by

T. G. Wendoe

Another project from **pickledog** *media*
Miami, Florida (U.S.A.)

ISBN 979-8-9879539-0-7
ISBN 979-8-9879539-1-4 (eBook)

We invest proceeds from our projects into efforts to foster the acceptance of people who look, behave or experience the world differently.

A debt of gratitude is owed to Dr. Michael Alessandri for his advice and encouragement, and to the outstanding team he leads at the University of Miami/Nova Southeastern University Center for Autism and Related Disabilities (UM/NSU CARD).

The pickledog team profusely thanks Albert Chavarria for his invaluable help making this project come to life.

The inspiration for this story is the amazing group of courageous dudes of the *Just For Dads* support group at UM/NSU CARD.
You know who you are. You are heroic.

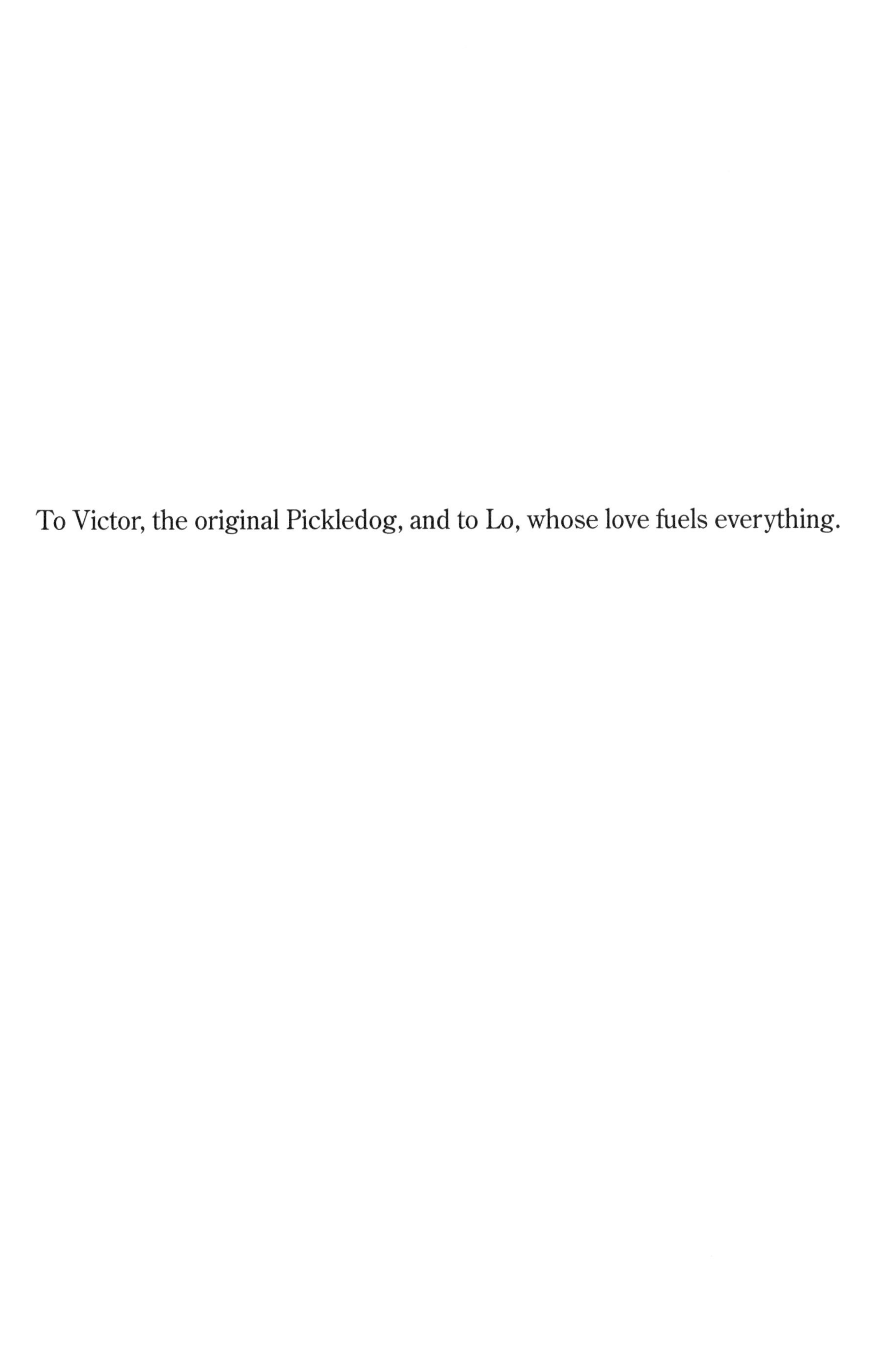

To Victor, the original Pickledog, and to Lo, whose love fuels everything.

Hello, kids of the world, how do you all do?

Did you come here today to delight in a tale of old mansions, venomous spiders and terrible ghouls?

If that's the case, I'll be your guide on this spookyful tour.

I'll be your host.

My first name is Usual, which is not very usual.

My full name is

Usual, the Unusual Ghost.

If you guessed that my job is to wander the halls of this house,

Sneaky as a snake.

Quiet as a mouse.

Using my ghostly appearance to terrify children and grownups alike,

Then I really must say that you're frighteningly right!

The duty of every great ghost is to sneak up on people and show them a close dose of terror and fright.

But the problem with being a ghost is that under my sheet
I am see-through to most.

I'm an invisible kid,

Trying my best

To be seen like the
rest.

I am most like a ghost when I go to my school.

I wander alone.
I have lunch on my own.
I don't have to be cool,
I don't set any trends.

I've learned to behave like
I'm my own best friend.

So, what is it about me that makes people stare,
At the way that I move or the way that I act ?

And why is it that kids seem so unaware,
That sometimes I wish I were less like a ghost...

...And a little bit more like a sociable cat?

What makes me unusual, if I do have to
tell,

Is that when I feel stressed I don't handle
it well.

    When I'm under stress,

    I tend to act out.

    And acting out always ends up in a trip
    to the principal's chair.

That's a quiet and relaxing place but,

Who wants to spend all day there?

That's why I wrote in this rhyme book for you,
A list of the things that make me upset,
And make me go **BOO**!

Imagine a bear, living alone in the woods.

Wandering around,
Listening to the birds sing.

Venturing out to find honey for food,
Hurrying away from the bees and their sting.

This peace-loving bear would be shocked
By the flickering lights,
And the hustle and bustle of a busy downtown.

    He would be drowned in the sounds of the
    crowds,
    And the engines of cars as they're driving
    around.

He would probably press on his ears
To shut out the noise,
And scream at the top of his voice:

    "I can't bear this no more!
    **Please take me back to the forest where
    I was before!"**

Vroom Vroom
Honk Honk
Screech

In more ways than one,
I am just like that bear.

Because I'm unusual,
Large crowds,
Bright lights,
And loud sounds

Are more than I am able to bear.

When you buy a new tee shirt,
Or jeans,
Or a dress,

Do the labels on them make you restless or vexed?

I have a **BIG** issue with labels I want to confess.

Labels are sticky.

Itchy.

Reckless.

    They scratch like sandpaper.

    They trouble my senses.

The tags on your clothes may be harmless to you,

    But to me they are terrible foes,

And feeling them poke never makes me feel good.

Dinner time is a happy time,
In the home of a kid ghost.

In our kitchen, we cook feasts and tasty roasts.

But don't think that every treat you love
Is going to feel good in a mouth such as mine.

Some dishes taste yum, but sometimes
The textures of food remind **me** of slime.

I hope that this rhyme has added to your education,
A sense for why unusual kids sometimes do
Unusual things that are quite strange to you.

Things that are caused by the stress or frustration of
Labels on trousers, shirts or skirts.
Bright lights and sounds so loud they hurt.

Big plates of food that look quite yummy
But in our mouths feel gooey or runny.

So the next time you meet a stressed kid
Who starts acting out,

Remember that a great many things you don't worry about,

Can be overwhelming to someone like me,
Who experiences life quite a bit differently.

So, go tell a grownup your friend needs attention,
Some time to calm down, some space, some affection.
Let's **ALL** help them go back to a less stressful place,
Where everyone is welcome to grow,
Welcome to learn, welcome to play,

Welcome to be there. Welcome to STAY.

Extra Knowledge for Curious Brains.

Autism is a condition that can make it difficult for some kids to be sociable or to make friends.

Kids with Autism can also be very sensitive to things around them, and sometimes they might react in unusual ways to how things sound, look, smell, taste or even feel.

Autism is not an illness. You can't catch it like you catch a cold or the flu. Scientists believe Autism is something you are born with.

You can really help a friend with autism by being kind and understanding of their unusual or unexpected behaviors.